"Buried Beneath the Words is a moving portrayal of how one woman's life was impacted by the weight of negative words and opinions. Betel's experience is shared with honesty and integrity, while laying her vulnerability on the line. Her narrative explores the power of words and how they impact our life choices and relationships. But, she reminds us that God's words are more powerful than man's words and can heal us and move us into meaningful and fulfilling relationships."

Yvonne S. Bogle
President of Women of
Worship Ministries

"Betel takes a witty yet impactful approach to reminding readers that they do not have to live their lives imprisoned by the hurtful things people say or have said. Not only does she encourage the reader to reject what is not in line with God's word, she shares a step-by-step plan for recognizing opportunities to embrace God's words and use them as a guide to a more successful and joyful life. Easy to read, fun, and potentially life changing!"

Erika Currier
Co-founder of Hope for Kids, Inc.

Buried Beneath the Words

A Young Woman's Journey of Embracing God's Word and Discovering Her True Self

Buried Beneath the Words

*A Young Woman's Journey of Embracing
God's Word and Discovering Her True Self*

Betel Arnold

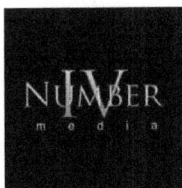

Buried Beneath the Words

Betel Arnold

Buried Beneath the Words

Edited by Valerie Utton

www.betelarnold.com

ISBN-13: 978-0986074400

ISBN-10: 0986074403

Printed in the United States of America

DEDICATION

To my children, Jeanne, Joseph, Billy, Jordan, and my step daughter Darianna. A mother always has her children in mind. "What will my children think?" In this work, I have you in mind. My wish is that I have learned my lessons and my desire is to always speak words of life and love to you.

To my mom, Ramona. Mom, all your life you have sacrificed for your children. You worked hard to raise us. Thank you. You are strong. Your strength helps me every day.

My siblings: Annery, Liz and Bryan—I couldn't have chosen a better bunch to grow up with.

To my hubby, Bill. How I cherish our times together, especially those long walks where I ramble on and on and you listen patiently and share your quiet wisdom—what a treasure.

Betel Arnold

ACKNOWLEDGEMENTS

Claire Hopley
T. Lak
Bill Corbett
Valerie Utton - editor and coach.
Valerie, thank you for your encouragement
and excellent attention to detail.

Betel Arnold

To those who are struggling:

It has been an honor to work with each of you. I especially remember the girls living in the hotels; the look in your eyes. I thought a lot about you as I wrote this book. I want you to know that GOD LOVES YOU. You matter. You are important. You have wonderful gifts inside of you. Don't believe everything the world tells you. Please give yourself a chance.

Betel Arnold

Contents

1   Buried Beneath the Words   1

2   My Winter Coat   13

3   Just Like My Daddy   21

4   "Hey… What Did I Do?"   33

5   The Joneses   43

6   "Van Para Atrás Como el Cangrejo"   53

7   Let's Break It Down   63

8   Every Journey Starts With a Single Step   77

9   Don't Quit   87

10 Let's Plant a Garden   93

11 Confessions   107

12 My Testimony   117

Betel Arnold

Foreword

"Sticks and stones can break my bones, but words will never hurt me." Most of us grew up reciting those words at least once. But when we're young and don't know how to make sense of the things people say, the words we hear have a way of seeping into our psyche and acting like a slow, invisible poison. The truth is, words can hurt us deeply.

Like a lot of people, I grew up hearing the same things over and over again. When I was young, I just figured the things people said must be true. I certainly didn't know I had a choice about believing them or not. Now I wonder how many of us are still walking around buried beneath the words that were spoken over us.

That's one of the reasons why this book really hits home. Betel shares her own experiences and describes how the wrong words subtly crept into her mind and came to dominate her thoughts and hinder her personal development. I found myself nodding my head in agreement with the stories because they happened to me too. The exact details were different, but the result was the same, the erosion of my self-esteem and self-confidence. Without any idea that there was a better way, I eventually ended up married to an abuser, trapped for 11 years.

It took me a long time to understand how I ended up in such a bad place. Now I know it wasn't just the result of all the negative things I heard growing up; it was also the fact that no one was there to help me challenge my belief in them. I wish I'd had a book like this when I was younger. It would have given me hope as well as the knowledge that there might be a better way.

I survived my domestic abuse, but a book like this has the potential of preventing it. Awareness is key, and this book is filled with words that will inspire "aha" moments for you, and give you the awareness necessary to know what NOT to believe.

Luzelenia Casanova
Author, *The Masquerade Is Over*
CEO Lifepath Solutions, LLC

"Be careful how you think, your life is shaped by your thoughts."

Proverbs 4:23 (TEV)

Betel Arnold

1.

Buried Beneath the Words

"I realize that I constantly put down my children," my friend said sadly.

I took a sip of my tea and listened.

"When I speak to someone about them, I never have anything nice to say. I don't know why I do it. It's terrible."

I stared at her. We are related and I knew exactly what she was talking about, but I didn't know what to say, so I didn't say anything.

"The other day someone asked me how my daughter was and I said she was a mess, that she sleeps in all day and NEVER picks up her room. And then I got on a roll talking about my son and how unmotivated and lazy he is. But I didn't point out that they're both good students, or any of the

1

other things they do right. Why do I do that," she bemoaned. "Why don't I ever have anything nice to say about them?"

She stared at me, her eyes pleading for an answer. I gulped my tea—my mouth was full.

After paying the check and walking out into the cold brisk day, her words still sounded in my ears. In the shower that evening, her words continued to play over and over in my head. Even in bed that night, I could not forget them.

That lunch date with my friend took place many years ago. The reason I remember it so vividly is because it became one of those "turning points" in life you hear about.

I kept hearing her words over and over because I identified with them. I did the same thing. I was forever pointing out the negative in people rather than talking about their good qualities.

Before our lunch, I don't think I was aware of how much I did it. But after lunch, I started hearing the negativity coming out of my own mouth and I began to examine my actions, my attitude, and the words I was speaking. I wanted to know why *I* concentrated on the negative.

One of the reasons I was so determined to understand why I was doing this, was because in 1997, I had accepted the Lord Jesus Christ as my Savior (see chapter 12). So I was already aware that my negative thoughts and critical attitude contradicted the word of God.

As I continued to study the scriptures, a lot of things began to change for the better in me. But now, all these years later, I realized there was still one area that needed a lot of work—my mouth!

I dove into the word of God and I became even more aware of the importance of words. Everywhere I turned, the scriptures admonished me to be careful of the words that came out of my mouth. Scrutinizing Genesis 1, the power of words finally rang home.

God's words brought the whole world and everything in it into existence. Every time I read Genesis 1, I am reminded of this.

God didn't build the world the way construction workers build a house. He didn't dig and plant it like a farmer cultivating land. He didn't cook it up like a parent making supper. **He said words** and His words had the power to make our whole world.

Genesis 1:27 tells us that we are made in God's image, so I knew human words were powerful too. I knew from my own experience that they can do terrible damage to people. I also knew they could heal and support us too. But I was still a long way from changing the words I used when I spoke about myself or others. I was even farther away from understanding the impact the words of others had on my life.

I prayed about this incessantly. I asked God to just cleanse my mouth. "Put a guard over my mouth Lord," I pleaded. Or as Psalm 141:3 puts it so well:

> *"Set a guard over my mouth, Lord; keep watch over the door of my lips."*

"Why won't you cleanse my mouth God?" I cried. "You could do anything." I desperately wanted to be that perfect Christian—the girl who never said anything negative, thought anything negative, and could do all things through Christ who strengthened her. Wasn't this what the scriptures taught? "A miracle, God," I prayed. "Do a miracle in me." I wanted to close my eyes and then poof! By osmosis, my mind would be renewed; my lips cleansed. Boy, was there a lesson in store for me.

God saved me. He sent His son to die for me. God shed things from my life. I no longer wanted to "drop it like it's hot" at the clubs, or go out and get drunk and act like a fool. I no longer needed the attention of men to feel beautiful, desirable, or wanted. I now had the "Daddy" I desired more than anything. I now had God.

God's word tells us that He is a Father to the fatherless, that He would never leave me nor forsake me. My heavenly Daddy accepted me; my name was written in His hand. Wow.

But I wanted desperately to change everything about myself quickly! "Now Lord!" I prayed.

Although I had accepted Jesus Christ as my Lord and Savior, I still felt insecure about my abilities. When I was around people, I would puff myself up. I was talking a good game, but when I was on my way home I'd think, "Geez what a prideful jerk I sounded like." My mouth was still like a dagger when I did not get my way. My husband can attest to that.

One day, my husband and I got into a huge argument. Despite my efforts to get there on time, we were going to be late for church. My

Buried Beneath the Words

insecurities ran deep. I wanted to show my church family that I had it all together, that I was the perfect, obedient, submissive wife, the ideal mother, the anointed Christian who was able to keep herself and her children looking the part, etc. Well, needless to say, that was a heavy burden on all of us.

I thought I had found the one place where I could succeed—church. All I had to do was follow the rules and I would be praised for having succeeded and excelled at something. The problem was, my family wouldn't do as I said.

The day we got into that huge argument happened to be a church day—Sunday. I was furious at my husband because we were going to be late and I felt like he was making me look bad in front of the "church" people. I had a certain image I wanted to uphold and I thought he had to make believe that we had the perfect marriage and the perfect family life.

When my husband told me to "chill out," I exploded. My mouth ran off and I said things I meant and things I didn't mean. I was cruel.

What had happened to my Christianity? I'll never forget what my husband said to me before he walked out the door, "What kind of Christian are you? Stay home. Don't bother going to all those meetings. For what? You're wasting your time."

His words were like a dagger in my heart. He was right! "God," I screamed, "Why can't you change me? Can't you just control my mouth? Puh-l-e-a-s-e," I sobbed and screamed. "Change me!" I demanded.

That was a long time ago. But here is what I have learned. There are things that are deeply ingrained in us—things we know about and things we are not so aware of. Change does not come overnight. Believe me, I wish it did. I would be the first one in line for a quick microwave pop. Zap! And there I'd be—a new me.

That's not how it works. Life is a journey. We are changed little by little. The changes that have occurred in my life have come from situations like the one I mentioned above; times when I failed miserably, times when my words and behavior have embarrassed me or let me down. Those situations have given me insight into how I think and operate. They have sharpened me and softened me too.

I believe God allowed all those trials in my life so that I could see my true self, see that although I

Buried Beneath the Words

was saved, I was trying to prove that I was valuable too. "Hey, look at me. Betel is somebody."

What God was trying to show me was that I was already somebody. More than that, that I was somebody loveable, accepted, and approved. I didn't have to accomplish something big and be admired by "the people" to gain self-worth. I already had worth. I just didn't know it.

It wasn't until I ended up on my floor sobbing time and time again after trying to impress people that I finally gave up. I could no longer do it. It was too hard. Pleasing and impressing people had worn me out and taken a toll on me, my children, my husband, and my faith.

I gave up and God moved in, saving me and showing me what was inside of me. He showed me that I had a wrong way of thinking, a pattern that had started early in my childhood. I was buried beneath the words I believed; words that had been used to describe me, my world, and my place in the world.

Those words shaped the way I thought and therefore the way I behaved. As old as they were, they were still alive in me and now they weren't just bad for me, they were bad for my family and the people around me too. That's how powerful words can be.

In my heart, I heard God speak to me, "Change the way you think." I did. This little book describes what I have uncovered about the power of words and how they can shape our beliefs, and where to look for help when the weight of all those words becomes too heavy.

What are the words you have heard people use to describe you? Write down as many words and phrases as you can think of. Put a star next to the ones you don't like.

_____

_____

_____

_____

_____

_____

_____

_____

_____

_____

_____

_____

_____

_____

_____

Betel Arnold

Think of the people in your life. What words or phrases do you use to describe others? Be honest with yourself and make sure to list all the negative words as well as the positive words.

_____

_____

_____

_____

_____

_____

_____

_____

_____

_____

_____

_____

_____

_____

_____

_____

_____

_____

_____

When you read the words and phrases that don't make you feel good, can you see how they might have shaped your life? Take each negative phrase and write down how it might have shaped your thoughts, actions, or beliefs about yourself.

_____

_____

_____

_____

_____

_____

_____

_____

_____

_____

_____

_____

_____

_____

_____

_____

_____

Betel Arnold

2.

My Winter Coat

"You are so stupid." If I had a dime for every time someone called me stupid, I'd be able to buy my dream home by the beach. I will still buy that summer home, but not with the money I received for being called stupid.

I can make light of it now, but stupid is one of those words that only seems innocent when it's compared to the rest of the put-you-down words in the dictionary. It isn't innocent. It's hateful. And when you hear people call you stupid for long enough, you start to believe it.

I believed it. Growing up, I believed I was stupid because that's what people said. Not inadequate, or silly, or not paying attention, but actually stupid. We all make "stupid" mistakes, but

I was called stupid; and I put on this word just like you would put on a winter coat before walking out into the cold. Stupid—that was me.

My sisters, on the other hand, were considered witty and intelligent. Growing up with them, I marveled at how decisive, strong, and independent they were.

As the eldest, my job was to make sure everyone behaved and did as they were told. I was extremely compliant. My thoughts were "Don't rock the boat, and do as you are told." If one of my sisters and I got into an argument, I would quickly back down and want to make friends again. I couldn't stand anyone being angry with me. Even if the person was wrong, I would apologize. One day, my mother noticed this and said, "That's because you're so stupid. You let people walk all over you."

My mother was right. In my desire to keep the peace I did allow people to take advantage of me. But I took it one step further. I accepted that I was stupid. From then on, this belief dominated my thoughts and hindered my personal development.

What really put the nail in the coffin was having to repeat 5th grade. My mother was a single parent who worked long hours to support us. As a result, she didn't have time to make sure we were doing our homework. So while she was busy working to feed us, I was busy socializing. I slacked on my homework and I never studied for tests because I was too busy with my friends. The consequence of not doing homework or studying for tests was staying back and having to repeat the 5th grade. Oh boy, was that humiliating!

I remember walking home from school with my mother on that last day when report cards where handed out. My mother patted me on the shoulder, acutely aware of my misery and embarrassment. She grabbed my hand and walked her stupid child home.

That sealed it for me. The following year while I was in 5th grade again, I decided to do my homework and study. The reward was excellent grades. I passed!

Even so, it took a long time for me to discard the belief that I was stupid. Many, many accomplishments later, I realized the coat of stupidity I had been wearing for years no longer fit. Not only did it not fit, it was weighing me down; a serious hindrance.

Merriam Webster's Dictionary defines stupid as: "not intelligent: having or showing a lack of ability to learn and understand things; not sensible or logical." We have all fit into this category once or twice in our lives (maybe more, I'm sure) but for me, I had taken this on as an identity. I was living under the power of the word stupid.

Betel Arnold

Look back at the list of negative words and phrases you listed at the end of chapter one. Now that you've had a chance to think about it, which ones might have held you back the most?

_____

_____

_____

_____

_____

_____

_____

_____

_____

_____

_____

_____

_____

_____

_____

_____

Make a list of words and phrases you wish you had heard instead.

_____

_____

_____

_____

_____

_____

_____

_____

_____

_____

_____

_____

_____

_____

_____

_____

_____

_____

Betel Arnold

Mind Overhaul

I went around feeling stupid, and like I couldn't differentiate between making good decisions and making bad decisions. I felt terribly inadequate. I thought "stupid" encompassed all my problems and described what I was like. Then I began to apply God's scriptures to my life. Here are a few I chew on to renew my mind.

Psalm 139:13-14: *"Oh yes, you shaped me first inside, then out; you formed me in my mother's womb. I thank you, High God— you're breathtaking! Body and soul, I am marvelously made!"*

Proverbs 4:5-9: *"Get wisdom; develop good judgment. Don't turn your back on wisdom, for she will protect you. Love her, and she will guard you. Getting wisdom is the wisest thing you can do! And whatever else you do, develop good judgment. If you prize wisdom, she will make you great. Embrace her, and she will honor you. She will place a lovely wreath on your head; she will present you with a beautiful crown."*

Buried Beneath the Words

James 1:5 *"If you need wisdom, ASK our generous God, and He will give it to you. He will not rebuke you for asking."*

Bottom line: God made us. We are the wondrous work of His hands. We should not be rejecting His wonderful masterpiece. We should be loving and accepting of ourselves. If it feels like you're struggling with something and could use some wisdom, all you have to do is ask God. He will give it to you without reproach. You don't have to be Miss-Goody-Two-Shoes to receive it. If we ask, He will give it to us.

I can now take off that heavy winter coat. The sun is shining.

3.

Just Like My Daddy

How many times have you heard "You're just like your mother!" or "You're just like your father!" When you hear those words, it's usually because you're doing something your parents don't like; very often something that reminds one parent of the other.

Growing up, I constantly heard, "You are just like your father." Trust me, that was not a good thing as far as everybody else was concerned. Again, if I had a dime for every time, I would have my beachfront home already. I had to get out from under the weight of this charge.

My parents divorced when I was very young. I was born in the Dominican Republic and when my father left for the United States I was a year

21

and a half old. I am told that before he left, I adored him. He fed me, bathed me, and put me to sleep.

I was too young to remember anything from those days and have always felt a great void not growing up with him. So when I was compared to him in a negative way, it hurt me deeply because I got the impression that being just like him was definitely not good.

Today, I have an okay relationship with my dad; probably the best I could have under the circumstances. And guess what? I am very much like my dad! Oh, gosh. I do behave in very similar ways to him. I am his daughter indeed.

For instance, we both agonize incessantly over making decisions. We are quick to make them, and quick to question whether we made the right one. Recently, I had a conversation with him. It went like this:

> Dad: "I booked a trip to the Dominican Republic. But now I don't think I should go. But your brother says I'm getting old and this is probably the last time I will see him."

Betel Arnold

Me: "He's right dad. You already booked the trip. You should go."

Dad: "But now I'm thinking about the travel. I might have to go up the stairs... and what's the weather like over there. . ."

Me: "Dad, you always go through this. After you make a decision, you always question it."

Dad: "Really? Are you like that?"

Me: "Yes Dad...unfortunately."

So after my dad cancelled his trip, he regretted it immediately and called me again.

Dad: "I was supposed to leave yesterday, but I cancelled my trip. I hurt my leg; I couldn't possibly travel like that. I shouldn't have cancelled though. I think I'm feeling better now."

Me: "Dad. You always feel like this. You should go. Once you arrive you will be glad you went. This is your process. This is normal for you. You always second-guess your decisions and get anxious. Just recognize it."

Dad: "So… I should go… right? I shouldn't have cancelled."

Me: "Yes Dad. Go. You'll be fine and once you're there, you'll be happy you went."

Do I second guess myself and agonize over my decisions? You bet I do and here's a great example. I have been taking college classes off and on for the past 19 years to get a two year degree. Sad—huh? Not really. During those years I was busy being a wife and a mom raising my children. Still, that's a long time.

In September 2013, I went to see my advisor and she asked me if I finally wanted to graduate. It turned out I only needed three more classes to get my degree. If I took them all in one semester, I'd graduate in 2014—20 years after taking my first class. I said yes and that's when my struggle began.

The classes I had picked were: biology—with a lab, statistics, and creative writing—my last elective. For me, those three classes were more like four because the biology lab took so much work. Statistics freaked me out.

Should I do it? Could I do it? I hadn't taken that many classes all at once in a long time. I asked every person I knew the same questions, "Do you think I'm making the right decision? Should I take that many classes together? What if I fail? What if the kids need me?" If you'd been around, I would have asked you for your opinion too. I asked everyone.

I swayed back and forth on a daily basis. One day I'd think "Yes, I can do this." The next day I'd decide I needed to drop something. What if I got sick? Ay, ay, ay—I needed to make up my mind already.

The day classes began, I went to my first statistics class. After, I stood in the hallway of the 5th floor walking back and forth. Yes, I thought. I would go and drop the class that followed statistics—biology. Everyone thinks I should. They all said the same things, "Why stress yourself out? Just take 1 class and then take the others the next semester. What's the hurry?"

"19 years—that's the hurry," my brain responded. Honestly, I must've walked towards the office to drop that class only to turn around at least three times. I started getting embarrassed. Could all the people around me tell that I was

Buried Beneath the Words

walking back and forth? I finally left the building without doing anything. Gosh, that was such a struggle for me and I continued to struggle for two weeks into the semester.

Finally, I decided I had made the right decision and would stick with taking all three classes in one semester. I'm really glad I did too. I'm staring at my diploma right now. It's on my writing desk right in front of me as I type this. 20 years? Who cares how long it took? Hey, I did it. And by the way, in case you're wondering, let me brag a bit. My final grades were: Statistics - A, Biology - A, Creative Writing - A.

Yes, we do tend to resemble our parents in one way or the other. We have their DNA after all. But just because I resembled my father in one way didn't mean I had ALL his negative traits.

Besides, didn't I display some of his good traits too—like his spirituality? My father told me about God. He is an elder in his church, and I am ALMOST like one—kidding.

What about this? My father forgives easily. He doesn't hold grudges. Hey, wait a minute; isn't that why I got called stupid? C'mon people give me a break. I am an individual after all.

But anyway, here I was, shrinking back, thinking something was wrong with me because I was "just like my daddy." Yes, you might have an annoying habit like one of your parents, but you can overcome anything if you recognize it as a problem and work at solving it. And besides, who's perfect?

In what ways might you have become like your father, mother, or other influential person in your life?

_____

_____

_____

_____

_____

_____

_____

_____

_____

_____

_____

_____

_____

_____

_____

_____

_____

Betel Arnold

If you could change something you now think
you learned from someone else, what would it be?

_____

_____

_____

_____

_____

_____

_____

_____

_____

_____

_____

_____

_____

_____

_____

_____

_____

_____

Mind Overhaul

Okay, so here's how I changed my thinking concerning this matter. The scriptures! The scriptures told me that although I am my father's daughter, I am created in my heavenly Father's image. God created me in *His* image. We are *all* created in the image of the Maker of the universe. How wonderful is that! Genesis 1:27 (NLT) tells us:

> *"Let us make man in our image. So God created human beings in his own image. In the image of God He created them; male and female He created them."*

Look at what Psalm 139:13-14 explains:

> *"You made all the delicate, inner parts of my body and knit me together in my mother's womb. Thank you for making me so wonderfully complex! Your workmanship is marvelous."*

When I read this scripture, I realized that God created me in a unique way. Like a Master Craftsman, He took His time. In my mother's womb, God knit together my form, my personality, my looks, and my preferences.

Betel Arnold

God wove each of us the same way, making us wonderfully complex, and there is no one else out there like you or me. We are each one of a kind! There are no knockoffs when it comes to God's unmatchable creativity!

Now I respect and admire the work of the Lord's hand instead of constantly finding fault with myself, comparing myself to others, or not valuing my uniqueness. I embrace who God made me to be.

As for those negative feelings I had about being compared to my father, I have made peace with them. Yes, I am like my father. I second guess myself countless times. But I have gotten better. Why? Because of what God's word says.

And by the way, I discovered that my indecision was fear. I was afraid to make mistakes. I did not trust my own ability to make a good decision.

But I can trust God. Look at Psalm 73:23-24, which also helped me. It says:

"Yet I still belong to you; you hold my right hand. You guide me with your counsel, leading me to a glorious destiny."

I can trust God to lead me. When I am wrong, or I make a mistake with a decision, I remember what Romans 8:28 says:

"God causes everything to work together for the good of those who love God."

Hey, I love the Lord. I'm His kid. He'll help me. And when I do make a mistake and my decisions are not the best, I remember that ALL things—the good, the bad, and the ugly, work together for good. I will learn something.

Aren't you glad you're "just like your Daddy" too? Hey... your heavenly Daddy, of course!

4.

"Hey... What Did I Do?"

"This is all your fault!" Have you ever felt responsible for something that you had nothing to do with? As a kid I did—often. Growing up, my siblings and I got in trouble no matter who did what. And, we all got piled into the "trouble wagon" together. There was no discrimination there.

After a while, an idea began to form in my mind. I had to control things. Why? Because no matter who did what, it seemed that **I** had something to do with it. Call the control board, "Betel's in charge."

I'll give you a silly example. Well silly now, but scary at the time because who wants to get in trouble, especially with an old-fashioned Dominican parent? We're not talking about me being sent to my room for a time-out.

Here's the deal: My younger sister decided she wanted to cut her hair. We were teenagers at this point, but I don't remember exactly how old we were. Obviously, she was old enough to go out on her own and do it. The style at the time was really, really short at the top, with a tail at the bottom.

Ugh, that's probably what people would say right now, but it was in fashion at the time. Well, my sister went off and got that done. When she came home, I was the first one to see her.

"Oh my God," I said. "*We* are going to be in so much trouble! When mom sees you, she's gonna kill you."

My sister responded with, "I don't care." (Did I mention she was the tough one?)

Well, when my mother saw my sister, she had a fit. "Your uncle is going to say that you're no good; that you're from the street!" (She said it in a lot more detail; I'm putting it nicely).

She was right. When my uncle saw my sister all hell broke loose. *We* were all in trouble. The wrath of that occasion lasted a long while. So long

Betel Arnold

in fact that I'm still talking and writing about it today!

So that's where my controlling ways got started. Look my friend, I decided I was through getting in trouble. That meant you couldn't get in trouble either. I was going to control as many situations as I could.

When I was in the midst of writing this book, I texted my brother and asked him about my controlling ways, how they affected him, and if there was an example I could use for my book.

Bro: How about the time I got into a fight and you guys started fighting with the kid?

Me: Can you recall one where you got pissed at me?

Bro: How about when you used to make me and my girlfriend stay in different rooms when we stayed with you.

Me: What? Weren't you a teenager then? I don't even remember her... So how were you supposed to stay in the same room, lol? Well did you ever feel you had to do what I said?

Bro: When it came to cleaning and
staying together wherever we went.

Me: Must've been tough, huh...

Bro: No, not at all. It was like listening to
Mom…but in English.

Get my drift? I wasn't their mother! Who did I think I was?

How did all this affect me? I agonized and stressed over every decision my siblings made. After all, I didn't want to get in trouble for what they did.

Old habits die hard, but I'm better in case you're asking. I realized my "Please don't rock the boat" song had been playing way too long. It was time to change the record. After all, how long could it remain at the top of the charts?

Betel Arnold

Make a list of situations when you feel like you have to be in control of what's going on.

_____

_____

_____

_____

_____

_____

_____

_____

_____

_____

_____

_____

_____

_____

_____

_____

_____

_____

Look at the list and write down the things you actually had control over.

_____

_____

_____

_____

_____

_____

_____

_____

_____

_____

_____

_____

_____

_____

_____

_____

_____

Mind Overhaul

One of the things I began to do was to read the Book of Proverbs. I tried to do it every day because honestly, I needed the wisdom the scriptures provided. Reading them was extremely freeing, especially when they were talking about responsibility. For so long, I assumed responsibility for things that were my fault, and for things that weren't. Ever hear of false responsibility? It's a bummer. And it's a heavy burden.

If you take a dive into proverbs with me you'll be amazed at what you find. Allow me to share two scriptures with you.

> *If someone has a hot temper, <u>Let him take the consequences</u>. If you get him out of trouble once, you will have to do it again.*
> *Proverbs 19:19*

> *Don't promise to be responsible for someone else's debts. If you should be unable to pay, they will take away even your bed.*
> *Proverbs 22:26-27*

See what I mean? Surely, the wisdom in proverbs will keep you out of a whole lot of

39

trouble; especially when it isn't your trouble, but someone else's.

And here's another thing, God will only hold us responsible for what we have done. That's what it says in Romans 2:6:

> *"He will judge everyone according to what they have done."*

Isn't that freeing? Here's another tidbit I have to share with you to keep this honest. Whenever there was a problem in my family, I saw myself as the go-to person. Wasn't that prideful? I could fix it—Me, old powerful controlling ME! I had all the answers.

The truth was, I was buried beneath the belief that if something went wrong, it was all my fault and I had to be the one to fix it. Thank goodness I was able to let go of that notion. If I hadn't, I'd still be buckling under its pressure.

Here are a couple of different translations of Galatians 6:5, (*NLT*) which also really helped me:

> *"For each is responsible for our own conduct."*

I really like how the Aramaic Bible says it:

> *"For every person will carry his own luggage."*

40

I like that. My luggage is heavy enough, and sometimes I don't even wanna carry that. Why carry anyone else's? Bag check… please.

This is my story,
This is my song,
Praising my Savior,
All the Day long...

5.

The Joneses

"What will people think?" I heard that one a whole lot growing up too. We lived in a building where the first floor residents knew what the third floor residents were doing. It was pretty intense.

In our New York City building appearances were of the utmost importance because what a person did or failed to do became gossip for the rest of the building. It didn't matter how hard you tried to keep something quiet; within a very short amount of time, everyone would be on alert.

So I had to care about what the Joneses next door thought or else I'd be forever classified. No coming back from that. I learned that what the Joneses thought was a big deal.

Recently, I asked my mother why this was so important to her when we were growing up. "Mom, why does it matter what other people think?"

My mother straightened her lovely red shirt. "Oh…si…si," she agreed. "Muy importante." She took a sip of her coffee and continued. "Once you get a bad reputation you're done. My father never let us hang out with anyone who didn't have a good reputation."

"Okay mom, but it wasn't just about behaviors that might give us a bad reputation. We stressed about what other people thought about EVERYTHING. Even the stupidest things."

"That's just how it is," she said.

I wanted to question her further, but she got into a spiel about a man she once fell in love with. She wasn't allowed to talk to him because of what her family thought. Oh well, I'd lost her to a reminiscence of lost love. But here's an example that makes my blood boil.

I went to the Dominican Republic to get dental work. You can't beat the prices, and my dentist is the best. She's beautiful, friendly, and the biggest perfectionist I know (which works well when she uses her perfectionism for the appearance of your teeth). And besides, you must have that beautiful smile; after all, what will the Joneses think?

Anyway, back to my trip. I have a cousin who always stays with us in my mother's house when we go back to the Dominican Republic. She is a beautiful soul but when she was young she was stricken with polio and it left her with a limp. The Joneses say that she is ugly.

I still have tons of relatives living in the Dominican Republic. One day I was talking to one of my aunts and I told her I was going to take my cousin with me to see my dentist. My aunt is very beautiful and always looks just so.

"What! Her? You can't take her."

"Why not?"

"You can't take her with you. You know how high class the dentist is. Your cousin limps and she is ugly."

I could see the anxiety written all over my aunt's face. I got it! It was those darn Joneses again.

In defense of my aunt, from her perspective she was right. Most people in the Dominican Republic still think this way. If you have a handicap, you have few friends and you fall into a

Buried Beneath the Words

lower category. You are de-valued.

Too extreme, right? Tell me about it. But the reality is that this kind of thing happens here too. I know because I have a son who is in a wheelchair. Thank goodness I worked on my "what will people think" complex. If I hadn't, I'd probably feel like I had to hide my son, or that we'd all have to move to Timbuktu just to get away from those Joneses.

I share this extreme example with you to let you know that "What will people think?" is alive and kicking.

I had that complex—bad! I couldn't be authentic. I was so concerned with what other people thought that the real me was buried. I had become a pleasing, do-the-right-thing fraud. Of course, that didn't mean I always did everything right (not by a long shot). But if people were watching, by golly, I tried.

Betel Arnold

When do you care about what other people think?

_____

_____

_____

_____

_____

_____

_____

_____

_____

_____

_____

_____

_____

_____

_____

_____

_____

_____

_____

What things have you always wanted to do but haven't because of other people's opinion?

_____

_____

_____

_____

_____

_____

_____

_____

_____

_____

_____

_____

_____

_____

_____

_____

_____

_____

What can you do today to start changing that?

_____

_____

_____

_____

_____

_____

_____

_____

_____

_____

_____

_____

_____

_____

_____

_____

_____

_____

Mind Overhaul

God doesn't care what the Joneses think. He tells us to ditch them. Proverbs 29:25 says:

"The fear of man lays a snare. But those who trust in God are safe."

I don't want to be like the leaders in Israel that John 12:42-43 talks about. They were afraid to confess their faith in Christ because of the Pharisees. They loved the praise of man more than the praise of God. No thank you! Keep that snare away!

I learned that man's praise doesn't last. Look at Hollywood. They raise their STARS and then Boop! Down they go; fickle, fickle people.

People will talk about us and judge us until we believe what they think and say. I'll take the advice that Apostle Peter gives us in Acts 5:29 instead:

"Obey God rather than Man."

When we obey God, we do not have to worry about what other people think or say.

God will not gossip about us. God won't blast our mistakes in the Enquirer, Star, or Sun magazines. What we say to God is between us and God. We can trust God and not have to worry about what other people say.

Buried Beneath the Words

"For as a man thinketh in his heart, So is he..."

Proverbs 23:7

6.

"Van Para Atrás Como el Cangrejo" (Always Going Backwards Like the Crab)

I like this one. "Nothing good ever happens to us," or "I have no luck." You might have heard it differently, but our favorite go-to phrase was: "Van para atrás como el cangrejo." Translation: "Always going backwards like the crab." (It sounds more exotic in Spanish).

Guess what, I believed this too. I always believed I was going backwards like that crab. I believed I'd never amount to anything and that whatever I did, it would either come to nothing, or I'd be worse off than when I started.

I believed these words. Yet, at the same time, I wondered why my family bought into them. After all, my mother's siblings had achieved some level of success. One of my uncles has been a successful business owner for as long as I can remember. One of my aunts was one of the first female teachers in her sleepy town of Gaspar Hernandez. A number of my uncles served in the military, worked in banks, and earned good pensions for their hard work.

My own mother showed us how hard work pays off. She has always been excellent at budgeting her money, and to me, she is one of the hardest working and smartest women I know.

So how did the phrase "Van para atrás como el cangrejo" become a part of my family? Does it really matter where the phrase came from or who started using it first? Not really. It's just a phrase my family always used to describe certain things, like a situation involving one of my cousins.

One of my uncles worked at one of the biggest banks in Santo Domingo, the famous Banco Popular, and was able to help my cousin get a job there. Well, my cousin worked at the bank for a while, but he became homesick for his quiet little town in the woods and quit. As far as my family was concerned, that was a classic crab move and they had a field day with it.

I've made my share of crab moves too, but there are two I will always especially regret.

First one: I had gone through the arduous process of applying for a job at a big insurance agency. It was THE company to work for. I had gone through two interviews and taken one long test. I passed both the interviews and the test.

At the same point in time, my first marriage was falling apart and I wanted to escape—to get away from it all. So when the company recruiter called and offered me the job, I turned it down.

Instead, I decided to embark on a different journey that led me down a different path. Maybe one day I'll write a book about that part of my journey, but for the sake of staying on topic, I'll just say it was definitely the wrong path. Trying to escape your problems is never the right solution.

The other example is one that's still an embarrassment to me today. I was still on that journey to get away, to escape, so I joined the Army Reserves. Well, since I was trying to escape, you would think that when my drill sergeant came to me and told me I had scored high enough on their tests to be part of their "fast-track" program, I would have parked my wandering behind.

Nope, not me. I wanted to walk alongside the other privates and smell the roses. Well, maybe not to smell the roses; there were no roses on that path, but I wanted to be a member of the group in every way. I didn't want to be singled out. Did I open the door when opportunity knocked? Heck no! That was too scary. What did I do? I quit.

Finally, I decided that for me, the crab had outlived its day. It was time for me to ditch it, especially if I wanted to succeed. No more quitting. Besides, success is in my DNA. Remember my heavenly Daddy? I am made in His image. I've got some good stuff in me.

Fast Track—here I come!

Betel Arnold

What slogans or sayings have you bought into hook, line, and sinker?

_____

_____

_____

_____

_____

_____

_____

_____

_____

_____

_____

_____

_____

_____

_____

_____

_____

_____

What do you think God would have to say about those slogans or sayings?

_____

_____

_____

_____

_____

_____

_____

_____

_____

_____

_____

_____

_____

_____

_____

_____

_____

Write yourself a new slogan or saying that will help you avoid falling into the "crab trap."

_____

_____

_____

_____

_____

_____

_____

_____

_____

_____

_____

_____

_____

_____

_____

_____

_____

_____

Mind Overhaul

Leave The Poor Crab Alone!

Shhhh... come closer. Let me tell you how I finally released the crab. I read about a man in Matthew 25, beginning in verse 14, who gave talents (money) to his servants, but he didn't give the same amount to each one of them. (I wonder how much he would have given me? Me, me, me, it's always about me, ugh!)

All right, here's what happened. The Scripture describes a man who was going on a journey. He calls his servants to talk to them before he leaves because he is entrusting his property to them. One of the things he does is distribute talents (money) between them, each according to their ability.

To one servant he gives five talents; to another he gives two talents; to another he gives one talent. Then he leaves.

The man who received five talents put his money to work at once and gained five more. The one who had two talents doubled his money too. But the one who had received one talent had dug a hole in the ground and buried the money.

When the master came back he congratulated the two servants who had gained, but he called the servant who had hidden his talent wicked and lazy. The servant had a ton of excuses like: "I was afraid" and "You were a hard man."

It was a classic crab move. He didn't have the courage to move forward, and all he had to show at the end was a bunch of excuses.

C'mon guys. Ditch the crab. Accomplishing anything takes work. Be willing to do the work.

Scripture confirms this, so before you confuse me for a preacher, I'll slip Proverbs 12:24 into the conversation:

"Work hard and you become a leader. Be lazy and you will become a slave."

Proverbs 14:23 tells us another truth:

"Hard work brings a profit, but mere talk leads to poverty."

See, it's not the crab's fault. Work hard and when opportunity knocks, you'll be ready to answer the door.

"For God's word is alive and active. Sharper than any two-edged sword..."

Hebrews 4:12

7.

Let's Break It Down

Why did I have such a hard time accomplishing anything? The answer is that I was buried beneath all the demeaning words and thoughts I've been telling you about. They were such an ordinary part of my life that they affected both what I believed about myself and what came out of my mouth.

The scriptures say that what is in you will come out of you.

> *"Out of the abundance of the heart, the mouth will speak."* Luke 6:45

My heart and mind were full of all those negative ideas that had grown out of everything people had said about me and to me. I was a prisoner, buried beneath the words that had shaped my beliefs about myself—beliefs built with words I had accepted as my reality without considering whether they were really true.

The sad part about all this was that I didn't realize this was the reason I acted as I did. I had been buried beneath so many words and beliefs for so long, that I couldn't see them. I thought they were normal. Instead, I kept trying to change myself. I didn't have any success because I didn't recognize the problem.

Has this happened to you? Do you say and do things and you aren't sure why? Maybe you're buried beneath false beliefs too. Maybe you've accepted the words you've heard about yourself as truth without realizing it and now they're manifesting in what you say and do.

Once I figured out that this was what was happening to me, I knew I had to start replacing all those negative words and beliefs about myself with more of God's words.

> Psalm 139:14 *"I am fearfully and wonderfully made."*
> Philippians 4:13 *"I can do all things through Christ who gives me strength."*

Betel Arnold

Deuteronomy 28:13 *"I am above only and never beneath."*

Romans 8:28 *"For I know that ALL things work for good to them that love the Lord."*

Psalm 27:3 *"Though an army encamp against me, I will not fear for God is with me."*

Psalm 27:13 *"I would have despaired had I not believed that I would see the goodness of the Lord in the land of the living."*

I went back to Genesis 1 to remind myself that God's words are powerful and life-giving. God spoke the world into existence with His words. And I knew I could trust that God's words would help me change my mindset and my deep beliefs about myself, and help me ditch my current vocab.

When I looked for more words to get in agreement with, I found the story of Ezekiel. Ezekiel was a prophet who received many visions from God, but there is one in particular that really caught my attention. It is the story of the "dry bones." In his vision, Ezekiel sees a valley full of dry bones—dead disconnected bones. When Ezekiel is confronted with this, God instructs him:

65

"Son of man, 'prophecy to the bones." (Prophecy means to speak or declare something that will happen in the future.)

Ezekiel begins to speak to the bones, and lo and behold, he begins to hear a rattling sound. The bones started coming to life. They begin to connect with each other, tendons connecting the bones, flesh covering them until an army—alive and revived, stood before Ezekiel because he had prophesied (spoken God's word) over the bones! Ezekiel spoke God's words to the bones; breath came into the bones, and the bones were revived.

When I read this story, it made me think about all the dead areas still hanging around in my own life. There were still times when I was an insecure, quit before you even begin, don't stick your neck out for anybody kind of gal. It wasn't just because I'd been buried under the weight of other people's words and beliefs about who I was; it was also because I'd been buried under the weight of the insecurities those words and beliefs had inspired in me.

I needed some of that life giving breath Ezekiel had spoken to those bones to be spoken to me. So, when I read that story in the bible, I was like "WOW! Can this really, really be true? If I

Betel Arnold

speak God's words over my life, will there actually be a change in me?" I kept looking for more words to get in alignment with because I wanted it to be true. Then, I came across a teaching by Joyce Meyer.

Joyce Meyer is one of my favorite preachers because she preaches on the power of the word. In one of her teachings, she explained that she had a list of confessions which focused on what she wanted to see manifest in her life according to God's word. When she began her ministry she would hide in her prayer closet and confess the word of God over herself and her situation.

I called her ministry and was sent a copy of her confessions which were about two and a half pages long. If you haven't figured it out by now, let me tell you, I am an extreme gal; all or nothing. Know what I did? I confessed morning, noon, and night. I confessed until I lost my voice. I confessed over and over again until I just about drove myself crazy, but my circumstances were still the same. Well, it did get a little bit better because I was so busy confessing, I didn't have much time left to nag or bark at anyone.

Part of the problem was that I didn't have a clear understanding of what confessing scriptures

67

over my life meant—and you might not either until I explain more about what confessions are.

Most people think a confession is when someone confesses to a crime, or confesses to a priest. But there is another definition. A confession can also be a formal statement of religious belief. When I refer to confessions here, I'm talking about confessing scriptures over my life, and putting my trust in God and what His words says about me.

When we speak the word of God out loud, we are confessing our faith and belief in God and His words.

So, if I was confessing God's words, they HAD to be true—right? The answer is yes, but did I really believe that God's words applied to me? We all want to believe what God says about us, but it's not like we hear His words spoken over us on a daily basis. (If we did, I wouldn't have had a reason to write this book!)

For example, one of my first confessions was "I am lovable." I knew that God's words said I was lovable, and I wanted this confession to be true, but I didn't feel lovable; I didn't have faith in what I was saying yet. Like many people, I'd heard so many negative things about myself that I was having a hard time believing what God said about me.

My list of confessions continued to grow though. I kept adding to it because there were a lot of things I wanted to change about myself and my life. After a while, I could tell that my confessions had become nothing but empty words. I still didn't feel good enough about myself to really believe the good things that God said about me. I was just reciting a list of words I wanted to believe about myself; words I wanted God to believe about me too.

There is no formula for confessing though; no trick. My faith simply needed to be in God and His ability to do the changing in me. I'm glad God let me experience that failure because it helped me realize how powerful faith can be. I hadn't been putting my faith in the right place. Instead, I had been putting it in my "list" rather than in God.

The bible says that faith comes by hearing, and hearing by the word of God. In other words, the more you hear the word of God, the more you'll begin to believe it. As I began to listen to the words I was confessing over myself, my faith did begin to increase. As soon as I started believing and having faith in God and in His word instead of my list, my mindset started to change too. God's words were doing the work in me and changing me. And even though I wasn't able to see it, He was uprooting the false beliefs I had about myself too.

I still have a list of confessions, but now my faith is in God and in His words. I'm still a work in progress too, but God has rewarded me with a keen awareness of my condition. He gives me His guidance and wisdom to renew my thinking. I now suffer less. I'm not perfect—nowhere near, but God is with me in this and He will be with you too as you begin to notice what you believe about yourself.

God will be there when you start shedding long-held ideas like: There is nothing good in you, you are not as valuable as other people, or that someone else is better looking and smarter than you are. God knows who you truly are and will support you on this journey.

Remember Ezekiel's story? When I first read it, I wanted to know if speaking God's words over my life would actually change me." Well, the answer is yes. As soon as I began trusting the power of God's words, just like Ezekiel had, I began to speak them and I began to revive too.

Betel Arnold

So seriously, stop knocking yourself down. You are a work in progress. Be patient. When you feel the weight of all those old words and deeds threatening to close in on you, again, trust God. Don't let the words and actions of others stand between you and God either. Get off your own back and let Him change you.

Meditate on God's word. Have faith in God's word. Digest God's word. Rely on God's word and your confession, your mouth, your words, and your heart will begin to line up with what God says about you. You will see a change.

When you think, "This is never going to happen," remember that the iPhone wasn't built in a day. How many centuries did it take for our technology to get to where it is now?

The joyful part of this is that I don't have to write the words or wait for a vision from God to speak His words. They are always available in the bible, in a church, or even on the internet. Why not on the internet? After all, God does work in mysterious ways.

Ezekiel's Story

The Valley of Dry Bones – Ezekiel 37: 1-14

37 The hand of the LORD was on me, and He brought me out by the Spirit of the LORD and set me in the middle of a valley; it was full of bones. [2] He led me back and forth among them, and I saw a great many bones on the floor of the valley, bones that were very dry. [3] He asked me, "Son of man, can these bones live?"

I said, "Sovereign LORD, you alone know."
[4] Then He said to me, "Prophesy to these bones and say to them, 'Dry bones, hear the word of the LORD! [5] This is what the Sovereign LORD says to these bones: I will make breath[a] enter you, and you will come to life. [6] I will attach tendons to you and make flesh come upon you and cover you with skin; I will put breath in you, and you will come to life. Then you will know that I am the LORD.'"

[7] So I prophesied as I was commanded. And as I was prophesying, there was a noise, a rattling sound, and the bones came together, bone to bone. [8] I looked, and tendons and flesh appeared on them and skin covered them, but there was no breath in them.

72

Betel Arnold

⁹ Then He said to me, "Prophesy to the breath; prophesy, son of man, and say to it, 'This is what the Sovereign LORD says: Come, breath, from the four winds and breathe into these slain, that they may live.'" ¹⁰ So I prophesied as he commanded me, and breath entered them; they came to life and stood up on their feet—a vast army.

¹¹ Then He said to me: "Son of man, these bones are the people of Israel. They say, 'Our bones are dried up and our hope is gone; we are cut off.' ¹²
Therefore prophesy and say to them: 'This is what the Sovereign LORD says: My people, I am going to open your graves and bring you up from them; I will bring you back to the land of Israel. ¹³ Then you, my people, will know that I am the LORD, when I open your graves and bring you up from them. ¹⁴ I will put my Spirit in you and you will live, and I will settle you in your own land. Then you will know that I the LORD have spoken, and I have done it, declares the LORD.'"

A New Day

One of my favorite things about God is that He is always there. We don't have to wait for God; God is waiting on us. One day, I just made the

73

choice to welcome His help. It's a choice you can make too.

When you commit to God and partner with Him to change the wrong beliefs you hold about yourself, your life will change. It doesn't always happen overnight, but there's a lot of comfort to be found in God's words as time goes by. He knows how heavy your coat of negative words is. All you have to do is give God the same chance He is giving you every second of every day of your life.

Think about the words that come out of your mouth and immediately reject them if they are not in line with God's word. If you commit to this, if you are diligent, it won't be long before you begin to accept the truth of God's word. Then the words that come out of your mouth will line up with the truth of who you are and you will begin to see a change.

Remember, your "Heavenly Daddy" is with you all the way! Now, start moving. Start living the life God wants you to live. And by the way...

BUY YOURSELF A NEW COAT!

Make a list of all the words, beliefs, and actions you are ready to get rid of.

_____

_____

_____

_____

_____

_____

_____

_____

_____

_____

_____

_____

_____

_____

_____

_____

_____

Betel Arnold

8.

Every Journey Starts With a Single Step

In the last chapter I explained that I had confessed over myself until my confessions got tired. That was true. My mistake had been thinking that the power was in my list and that all I had to do was say the words on my list over and over again, and then poof! I'd be changed. Then I realized I needed to have faith in the words because they were God's words.

Once I made that change, I progressed and started becoming more aware of myself and the situations I was getting myself into. And, I still definitely wanted to change. I wanted my life to reflect what God's words were saying about me so

I created a vision of what I wanted my life to be like. I wanted to be fearless. I wanted to be disciplined. I wanted to be organized. I wrote these things down on paper so they would always be there as reminders of my goals.

Wouldn't it be wonderful if I could just tell you how perfectly everything went after that? I guess I could, but that would be a lie. I wanted to believe that "failure wasn't an option," but it was. Don't get me wrong, there were changes for the better, but I still struggled with things that weren't changing and there were times when I'd felt so lost that I just about gave up.

Thankfully, God didn't give up on me. Instead, He helped me see that I was putting too much faith in *my* ability to choose a direction for my life. I was thinking to myself "If I just do these things, then I will become a better person, and then my life will turn out the way I want it to."

That wasn't where my faith belonged. It belonged in the knowledge that I was speaking God's words, and in the truth that faith in God and His words would come together to lead me through God's blueprint for my life. I had to trust that God was working in me through His word even when I didn't see it.

Broken

One situation I continued to struggle with had to do with "people pleasing." But like I said, I was still learning and here's what happened. When I started confessing about "people pleasing" it was because I wanted to get out from under the burden of always trying to make everybody else happy. It was exhausting.

By now, I knew there was an answer. I just hadn't found it yet. So where did I go? You guessed it—to God's words. As I read, I gained a better understanding of what it meant to trust that God was going to change me, and that I needed to truly put my faith in God's words and His ability.

> *"For am I now seeking the approval of man, or of God? Or am I trying to please man? If I were still trying to please man, I would not be a servant of Christ."*
>
> Galatians 1:10

This scripture was important because it told me that I had a choice between pleasing people and pleasing God. I realized that if I chose to please people, I would continue to struggle with what other people thought about me and what I was doing. I didn't want to do that anymore.

The solution? I decided to become a "God pleaser" instead of a "people pleaser." I found a confession and really started concentrating on it.

I began repeating that confession over and over, day and night. I must have said it over 100 times a day (which is a lot when you are a busy parent!). I started as soon as I got up in the morning and continued until I went to bed at night. Seriously, I heard that confession in my dreams.

Trust me when I tell you this; after about 3 days, I felt something break. It's unexplainable, but something broke within me. I felt it. It broke and I knew it was broken and gone forever. The feeling was so liberating.

It's not that I don't take other people's feeling into consideration while making a decision anymore, I do. But I am no longer a prisoner to other people's approval. God's approval is good enough for me.

One of the most liberating aspects of my new found freedom is that my decisions are no longer based on the fear of disapproval. They are based on being pleasing to God. My morals, belief system, and desire to be a good human being are based on the foundation of my faith.

Live your life in a way that makes sense to you; not to others. Let God's words and wisdom be your guide. Be true to yourself, respect yourself, and love yourself enough to value what you think. You will never regret it.

Most of us struggle (at least a little bit!) when we start something new. This exercise should help you find a good starting point for your journey with God.

Step 1: What do you recognize about your life that you'd like to change?

_____

_____

_____

_____

_____

_____

_____

_____

_____

_____

_____

_____

_____

Betel Arnold

Step 2: What do you want your life to look like?

_____

_____

_____

_____

_____

_____

_____

_____

_____

_____

_____

_____

_____

_____

_____

_____

_____

_____

Step 3: What Scriptures can you find that will work as part of your blueprint?

_____

_____

_____

_____

_____

_____

_____

_____

_____

_____

_____

_____

_____

_____

_____

_____

_____

_____

_____

Step 4: What will you do when you feel like you aren't meeting your own expectations or goals?

_____

_____

_____

_____

_____

_____

_____

_____

_____

_____

_____

_____

_____

_____

_____

_____

_____

_____

_____

*"Lord in You I move and breathe
And have my being..."*

Acts 17:28

Betel Arnold

9.

Don't Quit

Most of us give up too early and too easily. We make New Year's resolutions only to stop paying attention to them before January even ends. We go to the gym and then stop. We decide to wake up early to write, to pray, to study, to jog, or whatever. But when the alarm clock hits 5:00 a.m., we knock it off our nightstand. And then, instead of taking up our good plans for the day, we give up all together and say, "I can't do it. I'll never change."

Stop. Stop quitting. You can do this. You can achieve your goals. Don't give up. Quitting is never the right answer. You might change your course of action, find an alternate route, or simply modify, but quitting only leaves you feeling like a failure. Winners don't quit; they make it to the finish line.

I'll use Weight Watchers® as an example. I joined with one of my girlfriends. We were going to lose the weight by golly. We paid our fee and groaned about it the whole time. We made it easy on ourselves and signed up to have the meeting fees automatically deducted from our checking accounts, but we weren't happy about the deductions either.

My girlfriend and I got our packets and walked out the door fussing about the money. We put the tracking thingy they gave us in our purses and proceeded to go to Friendly's® to get the 2-2-2 breakfast deal—2 bacon slices, 2 pieces of French toasts (or 2 pancakes or 2 toast slices), and 2 eggs. Oh, and we added the home-fries for a few extra bucks.

We considered tracking the points for our meal as the Weight Watchers® lady had instructed, but we were too busy pouring syrup on our French toast. No tracking. We finished eating breakfast and then we just went home.

The next day, I took out my packet and examined it:

Betel Arnold

B. ARNOLD 07/24/2013
Weight: 151 lb. on Enrollment
Fee: $15.
Target weight loss goal: 10% less - 15 lbs.
Goal weight - 135 lbs.

"Okay," I thought, "I'll start tracking" and tracked everything I ate for that week. Here are the meeting results:

B. ARNOLD 07/31/2013
Weight: 145.4
Total lost: -5.6

Yeah! I was a happy camper. "This is easy. I can do this," I thought and decided to stop tracking. The next week:

B. ARNOLD 08/21/2013
Weight: 146.8
Total lost: -4.2

Bummer! Back to tracking.

B. ARNOLD 08/30/2013
Weight: 145.2
Total lost: -5.8

Yeah! Reached my 5 lb goal, but life got hard so I stopped tracking.

B. ARNOLD 09/06/2013
Weight: 145.6
B. ARNOLD 09/13/2013
Weight: 145
B. ARNOLD 09/20/2013
Weight: 144.6
B. ARNOLD 09/28/2013
Weight: 147.4

By this point, I was tired of paying the weekly fee. Then I remembered that if I became a lifetime member, I could attend all the meetings I wanted to without having to pay the weekly fee. To become a lifetime member, I had to set a weight goal and not go more than 2 pounds over that weight goal for six weeks. Easy right? Heck No!

If you look at my weekly results, you'll see that I was staying in the same ball park with my weight. I started to take the hint from my body. I might have wanted to be 135 lbs, but my body was saying something else. It was telling me that it liked the 140's.

So, I went back to Weight Watchers® and re-adjusted my target weight to 146 lbs. Remember, if I wanted to stop paying dues and end the automatic deductions, I could not go 2 pounds over my goal for 6 consecutive weeks. If I could do that, I would become a lifetime member—a "lifey."

B. ARNOLD 10/04/2013

Week 1 - 145.8
Week 2 – 145.6
Week 3 – 145.2
Week 4 – 145.4
Week 5 – 144.6
Week 6 – 146.4

Yeah! I made it! I'm a lifey and my wallet is happy. This is one of the simple, everyday examples I like so much. How does it fit in here? Since you ask, I'll tell.

If you notice, when I walked through the doors of Weight Watchers®, I wanted to lose 15 pounds. I had picked that figure out of the air because it sounded good and that's what I wanted. But I soon discovered that it wasn't the best goal for my body because my body had changed.

After weeks of not losing as much weight as I wanted to, and complaining about paying the fees, I RE-ADJUSTED my goal. I picked a goal I could succeed in reaching, and then I focused on maintaining that goal weight for 6 weeks in a row so I could stop paying meeting fees.

It took a total fourteen weeks. That may seem like a long time to lose only about 5 pounds, but if you were paying attention, I started with one goal but actually accomplished two goals.

1) I lost weight.

2) I became a lifey so I could stop paying the fees.

You might think this is a silly example (and it kind of is) but it isn't really about Weight Watchers®. It's an example of one of those times when you have a goal that you can't seem to reach. DO NOT GIVE UP! Check to see if something is wrong with the goal you have chosen. If there is, re-adjust. Once you re-adjust it, DO NOT GIVE UP!

I didn't give up and now I'm a lifey and I can go to Weight Watchers® whenever I want!

Betel Arnold

10.

Let's Plant a Garden

Words are seeds that will produce a harvest. Proverbs, 18:21 says:

"The tongue has the power of life and death, and those who love it will eat its fruit."

The word of God does not come back void. It will accomplish what it sets out to do. Think about your life like it's a garden. Think about the words that come out of your mouth as if each word is a seed ready to take root and grow because when those little seeds fall to the ground, sooner or later, they're going to grow. What seeds have you planted today? What will your harvest be? Will it nourish you or will you have to call 911 because it's killing you?

Planting our garden is serious business and we need to take it seriously if we want to make a change in our life. My hand is raised right now because I take this very seriously indeed.

Every time we open our mouth we are sowing seeds. As the words leave our mouth, they are planted, they grow, and they produce a great harvest that can either help us or destroy us.

A seed can lead you to victory or defeat. Any way you look at it, we are sowing our future with our words. With our words, we are speaking "life to our life," or "death to our life."

Do you know what seeds you are planting? Do you know what they will produce? Look at your life right now. Is it a mess? The evidence of what you've been planting is all around you, but you can choose what to plant in your garden from this day forward. Personally, I vote for words and seeds that will produce a good harvest—a good life. Think about the garden you want to grow. If you would like a healthy and productive garden, use these five steps as guidelines:

1. The Soil

The type of soil we plant our garden in can make the difference between a bountiful harvest or a famine. Soil provides an anchor for the roots of our plants. Soil provides food and key vitamins and minerals our plants need in order to grow and thrive. Without proper stability and nutrients, our plants would simply die.

Our soil is our faith in God. The only thing that pleases God is our faith. Hebrews 11:6:

> *"And without faith it is impossible to please God, because anyone who comes to Him must believe that He exists and that He rewards those who earnestly seek Him."*

As you continue on life's journey, you must believe that God travels with you, that He is always with you, and that He is the one who is going to do the changing.

It isn't up to you to do the changing, but it is up to you to be diligent about the process. You are the one who must have faith that the change will come.

In your past, you had faith in all those negative things you thought and believed about yourself. Now you know they were all false, and the time has come to replace those negative thoughts with positive ones.

To re-iterate; the first step is to believe that **GOD CAN—YOU MUST HAVE FAITH**. God is the only one that can create a real and lasting change in you. There is power in God's word. Believe in God's word. Believe in the power of God's word to create. Believe God's word can create a change in you. Okay? Okay. Next step.

2. Seeds

Words are the seeds we are going to plant. What words are we going to plant in our good soil? The truth about ourselves; what the word of God says about us:

> I am beautifully and wonderfully made.
> I am made in the image of God.
> God loves me.
> I have security with God.
> I am loveable. I am able.
> I am courageous.

These are all seeds that we are going to plant in our garden in order to get a harvest of success, confidence, and victory. These seeds are essential.

What if you don't know exactly what seeds to plant? Go to the word of God. Read His word. As you read, you will discover your true identity.

You'll have revelations, and misconceptions will be cleared. You will gain clarity about the words you should be speaking over your life. You will also discover wonderful stories and examples of people who felt fear, or who couldn't seem to get things right; and how God helped them—how God strengthened them.

You don't have to spend hours upon hours reading the bible. God knows the responsibilities you have in life. Read enough and enjoy reading His words. The bible is full of hip people, wise people, and foolish people. What a mixture of types! You'll find them all in there.

If you don't like to read, you can download God's word onto an iPod or a smart phone, find it on a CD, or watch a video. Find a way to listen to God's word. C'mon, you're creative; you can figure out a way to access God and His words. Explore His words and have faith and accept what they say about you. Let those words be the bountiful seeds you plant in your garden.

3. Watering the Soil

Water refreshes, heals, nourishes, and helps things grow. But you wouldn't drink just any kind of water. You'd want water that is pure, clean, and refreshing. So let's be choosy because the quality of the water we use to nourish our garden will help determine the quality of what it produces.

Let me give you an example. I used to watch true/reality TV because I've always been curious about how other people live. But, if you know those programs, you know that they also include swearing, fighting, and other questionable material. If I had continued to water my garden of thoughts and beliefs with all of that low quality input, it would eventually find its way into my own words, thoughts, and actions.

Trust me; once I started paying attention, I realized I wasn't doing myself any favors watering my mind with all the unhealthy stuff I was watching, listening to, and reading. Finally, I decided I wasn't going to let all that negative media pollute my garden anymore. Once you start paying attention, the same will be true for you too.

You want to start putting good stuff inside because what goes in is going to influence what comes flying out. We don't want to pollute our garden with poisoned water; and that's what all that unhealthy material is—poison. That's why investing in a bible, or a digital bible that you can listen to on an iPod or a CD or watch on a DVD is so important. Reading and listening to God's words is one of the best ways to water and nourish your mind.

4. Pulling Weeds

Every garden must be tended and yours is no exception. But no matter how good your intentions are, it's likely you'll have to deal with weeds. To help you with this task, there are a few things you should understand about where weeds come from and how to deal with them.

Your Words

The truth is that we have all been planting our gardens for a long time, so some of the weeds we are going to find will be the result of seeds we planted. How?

Here's an example of how it can happen. You are trying to be pro-active and diligent and motivated and have planted some good seeds in your garden. Then, one day you get up and feel lousy and start saying things to yourself like: I'm so lazy, I'm so un-motivated, and I'll never get anything done.

Sometimes you hear those negative words in your mind but it sounds almost like someone else is in your head saying them to you. Their words accuse you: "You're no good," "you'll never amount to anything," or "no one loves you." My friend, those are the kinds of words that grow into weeds.

Weeds can also be the result of words we've heard so often that they just hang out in our minds waiting for us to hit the 'replay' button. Every time we do, they become another weed in our garden.

I know that sounds scary because it's easy to say negative things without realizing you're doing it. And once it becomes a habit, it takes some work to drop. But don't fret. You may do a lot of weed pulling in the beginning, but once you start filling your garden with God's words, the weeds will get scarce. And, as with anything, practice makes perfect.

Start by listening to the words you use when you are thinking. As you begin to increase your awareness of the words that are running through your mind, you will begin to recognize which ones are *not* in line with God's words. The more you get used to thinking the right words, the less likely you are to say things that go against the person

Betel Arnold

God created you to be. And, the sooner you'll get the garden you've dreamed of.

Other People's Words

You must reject other people's words when they do not line up with what God says about you! This can be difficult at first because you may have never even thought about rejecting what other people say. Usually, if someone says something that hits us the wrong way, we don't say anything. When we don't, those words fall into our garden and produce weeds.

Why do they produce weeds? Because whether we believe it or not, once someone has spoken something over us that we have not rejected, it falls to the ground and germinates and produces weeds. We leave it there because we secretly wonder if what they said was true. Am I really like that? Am I? God knows what is true about you. Pull that weed out of your garden.

How do you deal with the people who are saying things to you that aren't in line with what God has told you? As soon as someone says something, politely say "I do not agree with that." And then tell them the truth of who you are in accordance with God's word.

It might be embarrassing at first. People might even look at you funny or tell you to "take a chill pill," but trust me, say it and you will be stopping those weeds from taking root in your garden. If you don't, your garden will continue to fill with other people's weedy words.

It's your garden. You get to decide.

The Enemy

The owners servants came to him and said, 'Sir, didn't you sow good seed in your field? Where then did the weeds come from?'
'An enemy did this,' he replied.

Matthew 13:27, 28

Don't be surprised to find weeds trying to take root in your garden even when you are making every effort to get and stay in alignment with God's word. The bible tells us they are the work of "an enemy." This is true. We do have an enemy—a true adversary—aka Satan.

This enemy's goal is to overrun your garden by planting seeds that will grow to cast doubt, dismiss, and destroy your belief in God and in His word to the point where there is no room left for God's words. Sometimes the enemy is hard to identify because the enemy is crafty.

Betel Arnold

For example, suppose you are hanging out with a group of people and everyone is cracking jokes and laughing, and then someone makes a joke about how lazy you are, or how fat or stupid you are. They think they're being funny and you'll probably laugh along with everyone else, but it isn't funny to you. You're trying to believe in what God says about you while the enemy is hiding behind someone else's words, trying to plant seeds of doubt in your garden.

The enemy's goal is also to get between you and God and it can happen even when you think you're paying attention to everything you're supposed to be paying attention to. You will know the enemy is around whenever you start to feel overwhelmed by doubt, fear, loneliness, despair, hopelessness, anxiety, etc.

All of those kinds of feelings are the enemy trying to get you to give up your belief and faith in God and in God's words. In fact, being aware of those feelings can help you recognize the enemy's influence rather than giving into it and looking for a person, place, or thing to blame.

The good news is that now you know. Whenever you feel any of those kinds of feelings, remember what they are trying to do; they are

Buried Beneath the Words

trying to choke the life out of God's words—out of God's truth about you, who you are, and your future. They can't. The only way the enemy's weeds can take root in your garden is if you lose faith in God's word.

Here are some things you can do when you feel the weight of the enemy pressing in:

- Saturate yourself with the word of God by reading the bible, listening to the bible, or watching something about God's word.
- Put on worship music.
- Listen to a sermon or simply go to church.
- Call a solid Christian who will encourage you with the word of God.
- Pray and ask for prayer.

Most importantly, remember that God is always with you. God will not abandon you. God will never lose faith in you or the true beauty of your garden.

5. Maintaining Your Garden

Once you start making progress with your garden, you'll need to remember to maintain it because there's no such thing as a maintenance free garden. And after all, you've done a lot of good work so far.

Maybe one of the most helpful things you can remember is that God is the Master Gardener. That means that as long as you are in alignment with His words, He will be there to guide you when it comes to knowing what to plant, when to plant it, when to prune, and when to harvest.

If you make a mistake and cut something you shouldn't have, let weeds take root, or forget about the garden altogether, it will be okay. Your first instinct might be to think "Oh no! I've deserted my garden and now it's out of control. I really blew it and now God's going to hate me because I deserted the garden He helped me plant."

That won't happen. God doesn't work that way. Whenever we sincerely and honestly ask God to forgive us, He does—no matter how many times we fall.

> *God is our refuge and strength, a very present help in trouble.* Psalm 46:1

I know it's hard to believe at first, but trust me, God will not abandon you. He has never abandoned me and He will never abandon you. God is always there to help you. He is there when you need Him the most. When you are at your worst, when you are most ashamed, when life really sucks, God is with you and He is ready to help you start your garden for the first time, or to help you restore the garden you've already started. Look for more scriptures to confirm this. There are so many you won't have to look very far.

For I am the LORD your God who takes hold of your right hand and says to you, Do not fear; I will help you.   Isaiah 41:13

God is always present and ready to help when you are in trouble. God doesn't want you to run away from Him, He wants you to run to Him. So please, understand that He will take hold of your right hand and walk alongside you. Let Him guide you with His words and His wisdom and your garden will flourish. That's scripture my friend.

11.

Confessions

Now that you have an idea of how to proceed, it's time to take a look at some examples of actual confessions. They are explained in Chapter 7, but just to remind you, the words of a confession are the truth based on God's word. Speaking the truth of God's words out loud is a confession of our faith in God and in His words. If you hear any words spoken over you contrary to this list, reject them. Only accept the truth of what God's word says about you.

Confessions are a part of my life—like breathing, but that doesn't mean I say hundreds of confessions a day. I don't have the time! It doesn't work like that anyway. I confess God's words so that my words and actions are in-line with God's blueprint for my life. My list changes because I'm always changing and I always need God's help.

It doesn't matter how young or old any of us is; we are all still changing and growing and will always need God's help.

This first list of confessions includes references so you can find them in a bible. The list that follows is the list of confessions I have spoken over the years.

God loves me so much that He died for me. John 3:16

I am the apple of God's eye.
Deuteronomy 32:10

The Lord formed me in my mother's womb; He knew me before I was born. He set me apart for His holy purpose. Jeremiah 1:5

Even if my mother and father abandon me, the Lord will never abandon me. Psalm 27:10

God is with me. He will never leave me or forsake me. Deuteronomy 31:6

The Lord has plans for me. Plans to prosper me and not harm me. Plans to give me a future filled with hope. Jeremiah 29:11

I put my trust in God and I will never be put to shame. Psalm 25:3

I am anxious for nothing because I pray about everything. I present my requests to God with thanksgiving and His peace floods my heart and my mind. Philippians 4:6-7

I will not worry about anything, for God takes care of all my needs. Matthew 6:25-34

I trust the Lord with all my heart and all my soul. I lean not on my own understanding. In all my ways I acknowledge Him and He will direct my path. Proverbs 3:5-6

With God all things are possible. Matthew 19:26

The Lord is my light and my salvation of whom shall I be afraid? Psalm 27:1

I will fear no evil for God is with me. Psalm 23:4

I overcome evil with good. Romans 12:21

In the day of trouble, the Lord will keep me safe.
Psalm 27:5

When my soul is feeling down, I do not rely on
my feelings. I remember my hope is in God.
Psalm 42:5-6

My hope is in God. I seek Him and He is good to
me. Lamentations 3:25

I love God and I have been called according to
His purpose. God works all things together for my
good. Romans 8:28

I can do all things through Christ who strengthens
me. Philippians 4:13

This is the day the Lord has made. I will rejoice
and be glad in it. Psalm 118:24

I commit my actions to the Lord and my plans
will succeed. Proverbs 16:3

I have hidden God's word in my heart that I may
not sin against Him. Psalm 119:11

God's word is a lamp to my feet and a light for my path. Psalm 119:105

I will wait for the Lord and gain new strength. I will mount up with wings as eagles. I will run and not get tired. I will walk and not become weary. Isaiah 40:31

I overcome evil with good. Romans 12:21

My Confessions

Without further ado, I will now share with you my long list of confessions. Do I have to? Ay... Yes! Sometimes I might change a word or two so that a confession fits better with how much our world has evolved, but I take special care to make sure that my changes are still in alignment with God's word.

You are free to use any of them. Just remember, when you say them, you are speaking the truth about yourself. They are God's words and because they are, they can give you life when you believe and confess your faith in them.

I am made in the image of God.
I am in perfect health.
I am whole.
I am free.
I am content.
I am peaceful.
I am strengthened.
I am joyful.
I am gentle.
I am fruitful.
I am stable.

I am determined.

I am diligent.

I am disciplined.

I am organized.

I am honest.

I am loyal.

I am kind.

I am trustworthy.

I live by faith.

I am a woman of integrity.

I am filled with God's grace, love, and mercy.

I have favor wherever I go.

I have hid God's Word in my heart.

God's Word heals me.

God's Word prospers in me.

God's Word delivers me.

I meditate on the Word.

I am a doer of the Word.

I am a teacher of the Word.

I speak the word.

My words are seasoned with salt.

I speak with grace.

The law of Kindness is in my mouth.

The law of truth is in my mouth.

I always do what I said I would do.

I finish what I start.

I always welcome and kiss my husband when he comes home. I give him peace and a wonderful welcome. My husband is the King of our home and he represents God. I treat him with honor and respect. My husband prospers in everything he puts his hands to.

I run my household with love, grace, and mercy. When my husband and my children come home I greet them with joy, love, and peace. God has given me a beautiful home. My home is a safe haven for my husband and children.

My children are healed, sealed, and delivered. I approve of my children. I respect my children. My children are married to Godly spouses. They are blessed.

The Lord gives me strength daily, hourly, and every minute.

I have seen the goodness of the Lord in the land of the living.

I trust the Lord with all my heart, all my mind, and all my soul.

I hear God's voice, and I obey it. I am led by the Holy Spirit.

Wisdom is my sister. She walks with me. I speak with wisdom. I listen to wisdom. Wisdom is my constant companion.

I am responsible with my finances. I pay cash for all things. All we own is paid for. I give. I have an overflow.

I commit my plans to the Lord and they succeed.

"Now the parable is this:
The seed is the word of God."

Luke 8:11

Betel Arnold

12.

My Testimony

On April 15, 1997, while taking a class at Springfield Technical Community College, I met my future husband Bill. At our initial encounter I played hardball. I wasn't interested. But my husband was (and still is) such a charmer that he convinced me to go out with him and I fell for him on our first date. By December of that same year, we were head over heels for each other.

Bill worked part-time doing sound and lighting for bands. On December 13, 1997, he asked me to go with him to one of his gigs—a Christmas Gospel Party at the University of Massachusetts.

It wasn't unusual for me to accompany Bill to one of his gigs—I liked going with him. We were in love and had even talked about getting married. It was the happiest time in my life, but that night I was exhausted and didn't want to go. Then, at the last minute, something inside me said "Go!" So I went.

When we arrived, I saw all these people jumping up and down and shouting the name of Jesus. They were praising God and talking about how good God was to them and how much they loved God. At that point in time neither Bill nor I attended any church so when I saw them, all I could think was "those people are crazy."

Bill got to work quickly but I didn't help him; I was too busy watching and judging. I don't know how long I stood there studying those people, but suddenly (and this is hard to explain or describe but I'll do my best), I felt like something opened up over me—like a light. I couldn't move. I tried but I couldn't. I was rooted to the spot. I looked up and I sensed—more than saw, this light. And suddenly, I felt like someone had taken a bucket and poured it over me.

That bucket was filled with love, peace, joy, anything that you can think of that is good. Someone took this "bucket" and they dumped it over my head and I was drenched, but not in

Betel Arnold

water!

I felt it flowing over the top of my head, covering me and filling me at the same time as it slowly moved down and through me all the way to the soles of my feet. I felt a transformation. I know this sounds crazy, but it's true. I felt it and I knew without a shred of doubt that God had touched me.

I felt transformed from the top of my head to the tips of my toes. I stood there, still unable to move—or maybe it was that I didn't want to move. Either way, I just stood there basking in the absolute delight of whatever it was that had touched me.

When I felt like I could move again, all I could think was "Oh my gosh, something just happened to me. God touched me."

I saw a guy standing in a corner and I ran to him. I grabbed his arm, repeating over and over again, "Something happened to me while I was standing over there. God touched me... God touched me." I was overwhelmed.

He was overwhelmed too and wasn't sure what to do with me. He said, "C'mon, follow me."

I followed him and he took me to a girl—Anna. I told Anna what had happened. I told her

God had touched me.

She explained that the Holy Spirit had touched me. I had no idea what she was talking about, but she opened her bible and pointed to one scripture after another.

"Read this one," she'd said. And then she'd flip through the pages stopping at another. "Read what it says here."

God knew what He was doing when He sent me to Anna. She knew her scriptures and used them to introduce me to God—God who loved me, God who forgave me, and God who was my Father.

She asked me, "Do you want to accept Jesus Christ as your Lord and Savior?

I replied without hesitation. "Yes."

"Are you completely sure? 100% sure?" She continued.

"Yes… yes." I replied. "I want to follow God from now on." And right there in the corner of a little room, I accepted Jesus Christ as my Lord and Savior.

Well, Bill was still working and had no idea what had happened to me. Driving back to Springfield, he asked "Why are you so quiet?"

"Bill, something happened to me back there.

120

God touched me."

"What are you talking about?"

"God touched me Bill."

"I'm not taking you to any more gospel events."

"Bill, I'm serious. God touched me. Something happened to me. And from now on, I'm following God. I'm not sleeping with you anymore, please bring me home."

Bill didn't know what to say. I could tell he wasn't happy and we drove the rest of the way in silence.

When I realized he was driving towards his apartment I said, "Bill, I'm not spending the night with you. I'm serious. Take me home."

"What's wrong with you?"

"God touched me, and from now on, I'm following God.

Bill thought I was crazy and I kind of understood. Who wouldn't? He couldn't believe what was happening. He kept trying to talk to me to get me to explain what was going on, but I just kept repeating the same thing—that God had touched me. By the time he'd dropped me off at my house, he was just plain mad.

I on the other hand, was joyful. I was

121

exhilarated. I can't explain the depth of the love I felt for God at that moment because words can't aptly describe it. I have never felt the intensity of that since. At that moment in time, I honestly did not care that Bill was mad. I loved Bill, but at that moment, I loved God more. When I got home, I laid down and fell asleep feeling happier than I had ever felt in my life.

When I got up the next morning, I pulled the business card Anna had given me from my purse. On it was the name and phone number of a pastor she knew. I called him and explained what had happened to me. He said it was the Holy Spirit and that I was welcome to come to his church in Holyoke if I wanted. He also mentioned some other churches, but it didn't matter to me where I went. I just wanted to follow God. After our conversation, he came over to my house and I started attending his church.

Bill on the other hand was not talking to me. He didn't call, and he didn't come around. You have to understand, that from the day Bill and I went on our first date, we had spent every single day together. We were in love. We wanted to get married. But since that night at UMASS, Bill had not called me.

Betel Arnold

One day, Bill's grandparents came over my house looking for Bill. They knew we usually spent every day together, so they came to my house looking for him. When they arrived and asked for Bill—words flew out of my mouth before I could stop them.

"Bill doesn't want to be with me because I'm not going to sleep with him anymore." I couldn't believe I had just blurted it out like that!

They were taken aback—but not for long. Bill's grandfather told me to get in their car. I got in their car and we drove to Bill's apartment. We went upstairs and Bill's grandfather told him to get in the car and then he drove us all to Friendly's.

His grandfather motioned for us to sit alone in a booth and talk. We sat there like zombies, just doing what his grandfather said. Eventually, we started talking.

Bill looked at me and said, "I don't know who you are anymore. I fell in love with a girl that looks like you, but I don't know who you are. I drive to a gig with a girl and I bring home someone who's different. I don't know you. I don't know what's happened."

I looked at him and I knew that what he was saying was true. I was not the same girl. In an

Buried Beneath the Words

instant God had changed me. But what could I do? There was nothing I could do.

I told him I understood what he was feeling, but that there was nothing I could do about it. I told him that I was going to follow God and that if he wanted to follow me that was fine, but if he didn't, there was nothing I could do. Understand me here; I loved Bill. I wanted to marry Bill, but I loved God more.

I chose God. But God was so good to me that eventually he brought Bill along and we got married.

Today

I can gladly say that I am no longer buried beneath the wrong words. I am under new words—God's words, and being under His words has released me and given me the courage to explore the potential within me. If I had not discovered that I was buried under all those negative words and carrying the weight of all those false beliefs, I would still be that same insecure young girl. Those wrong words were the reason I wasn't stepping up and doing the things I needed to do—the things I dreamed of doing.

Today, secure in my faith and my foundation of God's word, I have stepped out boldly. I am an author. I am the founder of Courage Under Fire Coaching which helps women find their hidden potential. I now help women uncover the real person that's been hidden or buried beneath the weight of the negative words and false beliefs they've been living with.

I am the co-founder and co-producer of the TV talk show Simply Talking. This show helps women become all they were meant to be by highlighting and discussing different areas in their everyday lives. Most importantly, I am a wife and

125

mother, and very happy with being both.

Thank you so much for embarking on this journey with me. It means a lot to me that you've taken the time to read my story.

My hope is that you will consider what I've shared with you in this book. There really is an answer for just about any situation or dilemma in God's word. Research it for yourself and come to the conclusion that the truth is there for you too.

You are worth it. Believe in yourself, find your true identity in God's word and reach your full potential. I will be thinking of you as you begin your own journeys.

Many Blessings,
Betel

On my Desk

On my desk I keep some verses that help me when things seem hard and I need a lift. I am including them here hoping they will help you too!

Don't Quit

When things go wrong, as they sometimes will,
When the road you're trudging seems all uphill,
When the funds are low and the debts are high,
And you want to smile, but you have to sigh,
When care is pressing you down a bit,
Rest, if you must, but don't you quit.

Life is queer with its twists and turns,
As every one of us sometimes learns,
And many a failure turns about,
When he might have won had he stuck it out;
Don't give up though the pace seems slow–
You may succeed with another blow.

Often the goal is nearer than
It seems to a faint and faltering man,
Often the struggler has given up,
When he might have captured the victor's cup,

And he learned too late when the night slipped down,
How close he was to the golden crown.

Success is failure turned inside out–
The silver tint of the clouds of doubt,
And you never can tell how close you are,
It may be near when it seems so far,
So stick to the fight when you're hardest hit–
It's when things seem worst that you mustn't quit.

- Author unknown

Betel Arnold

Consider Him

When the storm is raging high,
When the tempest rends the sky,
When my eyes with tears are dim,
Then, my soul, consider Him.

When my plans are in the dust,
When my dearest hopes are crushed,
When is passed each foolish whim,
Then, my soul, consider Him.

When with dearest friends I part,
When deep sorrow fills my heart,
When pain racks each weary limb,
Then, my soul, consider Him.

When I track my weary way,
When fresh trials come each day,
When my faith and hope are dim,
Then, my soul, consider Him.

Clouds or sunshine, dark or bright,
Evening shades or morning light,
When my cup flows o'er the brim,
Then, my soul, consider Him.

- Author Unknown

130

Isaiah 41:10 (AMP)

"Fear not [there is nothing to fear], for I am with you; do not look around you in terror and be dismayed, for I am your God. I will strengthen and harden you to difficulties, yes, I will help you; yes, I will hold you up and retain you with My [victorious] right hand of rightness and justice."

Betel Arnold

"I ran and ran and ran every day, and I acquired this sense of determination, this sense of spirit that I would never, never give up, no matter what else happened."

Wilma Rudolph

Betel Arnold

"... And remember, I am with you each and every day until the end of time."

Matthew 28:20

www.ingramcontent.com/pod-product-compliance
Lightning Source LLC
Chambersburg PA
CBHW071001040426
42443CB00007B/607